# THE DEMOCRATIC PARTY

## America's Oldest Party

by Dale Anderson

# THE DEMOCRATIC PARTY

## America's Oldest Party

by Dale Anderson

Content Adviser: Tom Lansford, Ph.D., Assistant Dean and Associate Professor of Political Science, College of Arts and Letters, University of Southern Mississippi

Reading Adviser: Katie Van Sluys, Ph.D., School of Education, DePaul University

Compass Point Books ✦ Minneapolis, Minnesota

## THE DEMOCRATIC PARTY

### ✦ COMPASS POINT BOOKS

3109 West 50th Street, #115
Minneapolis, MN 55410

yA 324.2736
AND

Visit Compass Point Books on the Internet at
*www.compasspointbooks.com*
or e-mail your request to
*custserv@compasspointbooks.com*

For Compass Point Books
Jennifer VanVoorst, Jaime Martens, XNR Productions, Inc.,
Catherine Neitge, Keith Griffin, and Carol Jones


Produced by White-Thomson Publishing Ltd.

For White-Thomson Publishing
Stephen White-Thomson, Susan Crean, Amy Sparks,
Tinstar Design Ltd., Tom Lansford, Peggy Bresnick Kendler,
Will Hare, and Timothy Griffin


The Democratic Party's donkey logo used with permission of the
Democratic National Committee.


**Library of Congress Cataloging-in-Publication Data**
Anderson, Dale, 1953–
    The Democratic Party : America's oldest party / by Dale Anderson.
        p. cm. — (Snapshots in history)
    Includes bibliographical references and index.
    ISBN-13: 978-0-7565-2450-0 (library binding)
    ISBN-10: 0-7565-2450-4 (library binding)
    ISBN-13: 978-0-7565-3169-0 (paperback)
    ISBN-10: 0-7565-3169-1 (paperback)
    1.  Democratic Party (U.S.)—History—Juvenile literature. 2.  United
States—Politics and government—Juvenile literature. I. Title. II.
Series.
    JK2316.A63 2007
    324.2736—dc22                                    2006034097

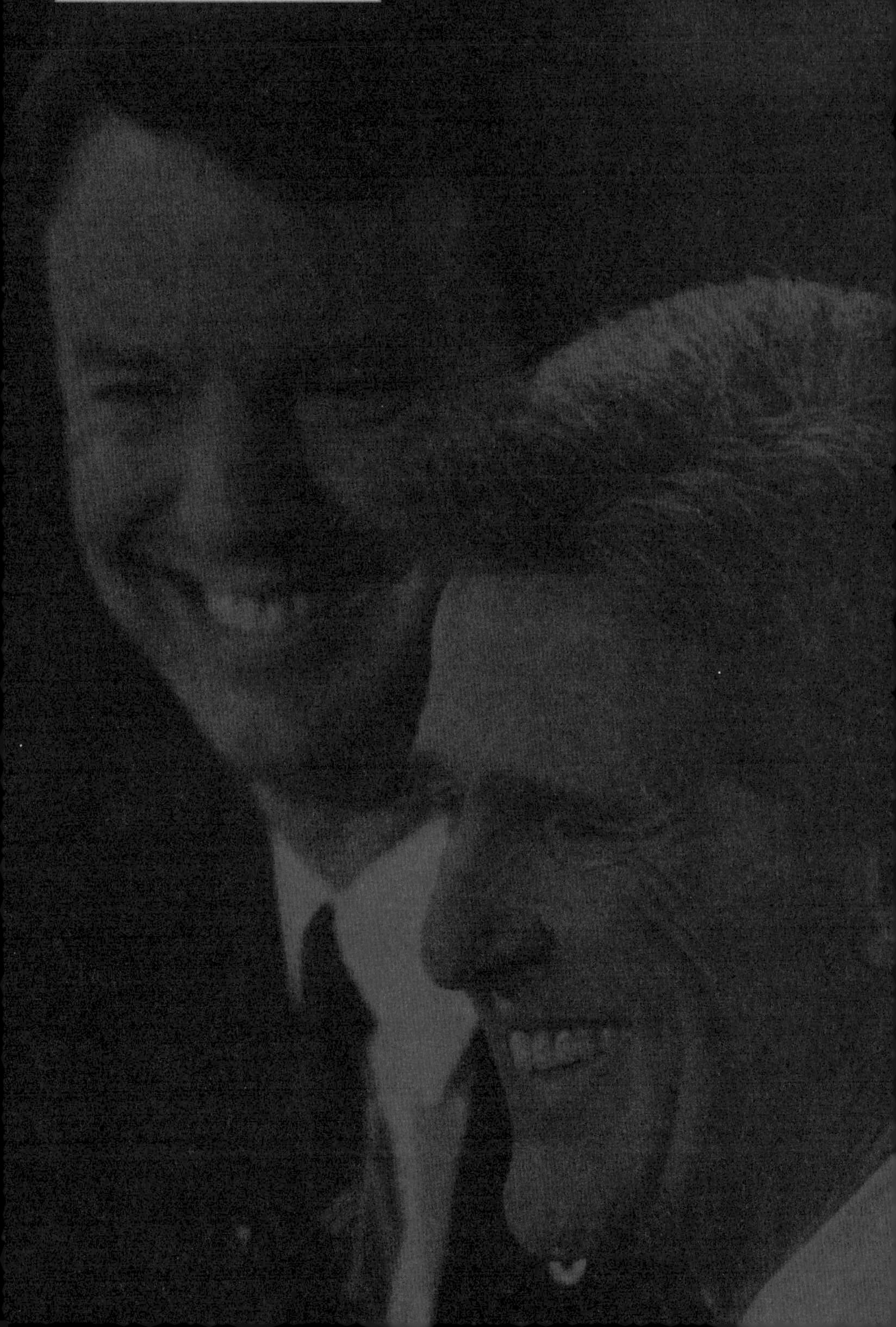

# CONTENTS

# Disaster in Chicago

The Democratic Party has seen many fractures and divisions in its long history. One of the worst came in 1968.

The turmoil began in New Hampshire, site of the nation's first presidential primary. Senator Eugene McCarthy of Minnesota was seeking the Democratic nomination for president. He faced a difficult task, because he was running against Lyndon B. Johnson, the sitting president, who had won the presidency in 1964 in a landslide.

McCarthy had a clear message: The war in Vietnam was a disaster, and President Johnson, who had committed American power there, was to blame. Thousands of American soldiers were being killed each year, and there was no hope of victory. Helping McCarthy deliver this message were a few thousand college students who had come to New Hampshire to promote his campaign. They knocked on doors, handed out pamphlets, and made phone calls in their effort to convince voters that it was time to end the bloody war.

*Minnesota Senator Eugene McCarthy was not well-known when he began his 1968 campaign to unseat President Lyndon Johnson.*

On March 12, New Hampshire Democrats voted, and their decision stunned the nation. McCarthy, the cash-strapped challenger, won nearly 42 percent of the vote. Johnson won the primary election with just under 50 percent, but his narrow victory was a major rebuke of his war policy.

The results sent shock waves through the Democratic Party. Within days, Senator Robert F. Kennedy of New York announced that he, too, would seek the Democratic nomination. This posed a serious challenge not only to Johnson but also to McCarthy, since Kennedy could also capture antiwar votes. A McCarthy supporter expressed the campaign staff's bitterness:

> *We woke up after the New Hampshire primary, like it was Christmas Day. And when we went down to the tree, we found Bobby Kennedy had stolen our Christmas presents.*

On March 31 came an even bigger jolt. In a television address, President Johnson announced that he would cease bombing parts of North Vietnam in an effort to encourage the Communist leaders there to begin peace talks. He ended his speech with a shocking announcement:

> *I have concluded that I should not permit the presidency to become involved in the partisan divisions that are developing in this political year. Accordingly, I shall not seek and I will not accept the nomination of my party for another term as your president.*

Soon after, Johnson's vice president, Hubert Humphrey, entered the race. He, like McCarthy, had served in the U.S. Senate from Minnesota. After several more primaries, none of which Humphrey won, tragedy struck. Early in the morning of June 5, Robert Kennedy was shot by an assassin. He died the following day.

In late August, a grim Democratic Party gathered in Chicago to pick the party's presidential candidate at its national convention. Several hundred peace activists also streamed into the city. They planned to protest the war and, if possible, carry their protests into the convention hall itself. The city's mayor, Richard J. Daley—a powerful figure in the Democratic Party—was equally determined to block any attempt to disrupt the convention. Daley prepared the city's large police force to stop the protests.

*Senator Robert F. Kennedy was shot by an assassin just after winning the California primary election.*

11

In addition to the Vietnam War, the party was split over the issue of civil rights. Two sets of delegates came to Chicago from several Southern states. One set was composed of whites who wanted to block any further advances in civil rights for African-Americans and retain whites' iron grip on political power in the South. The other was a mix of African-Americans and whites who were dedicated to promoting equal rights for African-Americans.

On August 26, the convention opened, and members quickly started fighting about which delegates to seat from the Southern states. The fight dragged on until nearly 3 o'clock the next morning, when the exhausted delegates finally

*Antiwar delegates to the 1968 Democratic National Convention used every opportunity to declare their opposition to the Vietnam War.*

adjourned. In the end, the all-white delegations were admitted from every state but one. The next night, the delegates debated the platform, and once again, angry disagreements pushed the convention into the early morning hours.

Wednesday, August 28, 1968, became one of the worst days in Democratic Party history. Inside the convention hall, delegates finally voted on the platform, approving language that supported President Johnson's actions in the war. The peace delegates howled in anger and disapproval. Meanwhile, the protesters began to march toward the convention hall. They were met by Chicago police, who used tear gas and night sticks to push the protesters away. The police tossed scores of people into police wagons while the protesters threw bottles and rocks and called the police "pigs" and "Nazis." It was a dramatic and ugly scene—and one caught by television news cameras.

It took more than an hour for the networks to process this film. When it was finally ready, they began showing it—just as Hubert Humphrey was being nominated. Together, the two scenes made the candidate look as if he supported the brutality, even though he had nothing to do with it.

Seeing the footage, the antiwar delegates demanded that the convention adjourn, but party leaders refused. Just before midnight, the roll-call vote was completed, and Humphrey was declared the winner. Bitter delegates left the hall.

A Chicago police officer addressed an antiwar protester bleeding from an earlier confrontation.

The next night, the convention endorsed Humphrey's pick of Senator Edmund Muskie of Maine as his running mate. Humphrey tried to heal the party's wounds with his acceptance speech, but his praise of President Johnson was met with jeers and his position on Vietnam with boos.

The candidate of a fractured party, Humphrey himself was crestfallen. He recalled his feelings:

> I was a victim of that convention as much as a man getting the … flu. … I could've beaten the Republicans any time—but it's difficult to take on the Republicans and fight a guerrilla war in your own party at the same time. Chicago was

## PARTY DISCIPLINE

The 1968 convention was not the only Democratic convention marred by deep divisions. Such splits are much more rare among Republicans. Republicans tend to bury their disagreements when it comes time to nominate a candidate. They typically follow what Republican President Ronald Reagan called the 11th commandment of Republicans: Thou shalt not speak ill of other Republicans. Democrats, however, are much more likely to fall into turmoil. This tendency prompted comic Will Rogers to say, "I don't belong to an organized political party. I'm a Democrat."

*a catastrophe. My wife and I went home heart-broken, battered and beaten. I told her I felt just like we had been in a shipwreck.*

Nevertheless, Humphrey was the Democratic Party's presidential nominee, and he now faced challenges outside his own party. Humphrey's main challenger was former Vice President Richard Nixon. A shrewd campaigner, Nixon had three main messages. He said he would end American involvement in the Vietnam War, although he never explained how. He promised to bring law and order to the country. And he sought the support of ordinary Americans who worked hard, paid their taxes, supported their country, and did not protest—people he called the silent majority.

Adding another threat to Humphrey's campaign was former Governor George C. Wallace of Alabama. Wallace set up a third-party movement called the American Independent Party.

*During the 1968 campaign for the presidency, Vice President Hubert Humphrey, the Democratic nominee, often had to plead with hecklers in the crowd to give him a chance to make his speeches.*

Wallace's campaign played on the anger of Southern whites over the end of segregation and on concerns of Northern whites that advances by African-Americans could endanger their jobs and schools. Wallace stood to make gains among traditional Democratic voters in the South and among unionized workers in the North—gains that could cost Humphrey the election.

In public opinion polls, Humphrey trailed throughout the fall. On September 30, in a nationally televised speech, he expressed his willingness to halt the bombing of North Vietnam in the hope of advancing peace talks. Humphrey's new policy was enough to energize many Democrats who wanted to end the war, especially since they feared both Nixon and Wallace.

In the last weeks of the campaign, Humphrey steadily rose in the polls, but it was too little, too late. On November 5, Nixon won 31.7 million popular votes to Humphrey's 30.9 million, a narrow win. In electoral votes, however, Nixon won an easy victory by taking 301 of 538. Wallace finished a distant third, though he won the electoral votes of five Southern states.

## ELECTORAL VOTES

The president and vice president are not elected by voters but by electors. Most states award all their electoral votes to the candidate who wins the popular vote. The candidate with the majority of electoral votes then becomes president. These votes are not automatically registered, however. Special people called electors cast these ballots.

The 1968 election marked one of the low points in the long history of the Democratic Party. Democrats had long seen themselves as the party of the people, the champion of ordinary Americans. But now millions of people were rejecting the war being led by a Democratic president, and millions from the silent majority had chosen the Republican candidate as their champion. Of course, this was not the first time the Democrats had faced defeat. The Democrats were the oldest political party in the United States, and they had seen their share of problems in their long history.

# The Origins of the Democratic Party

Chapter

2

When the United States was founded, the new nation had no political parties. Leaders disagreed on certain issues, to be sure, but they did not organize themselves into groups to actively promote a particular set of policies or candidates.

During the eight years that George Washington served as the first president, however, the first parties developed. One of those parties was the group that eventually evolved into the Democratic Party. At the time, one group of politicians favored a strong federal government. Their leader was Alexander Hamilton, who served as Washington's secretary of the treasury. Hamilton and his supporters believed that a strong central government was needed to promote American economic growth.

*George Washington, the nation's first president, worried that the development of political parties would weaken the government.*

They tended to be strongest in the states of the Northeast and were generally backed by men of property and those who owned businesses in trade and manufacturing. They also wanted close ties to Britain, the country's main trading partner. Hamilton and his supporters came to be called Federalists.

Others disagreed with the Federalist position. Thomas Jefferson, author of the Declaration of Independence and Washington's secretary of state, led this group. Jefferson and his supporters wanted stronger state governments and a weaker federal government. They pushed for laws that favored

*Benjamin Franklin (left) and John Adams (center) review a draft of the Declaration of Independence, written by Thomas Jefferson (right).*

farmers rather than businesses owners, and they wanted close ties to France, which had been a key ally during the American Revolution.

In 1792, Jefferson organized regular meetings with like-minded members of the U.S. Congress. In these meetings, called caucuses, they discussed how to advance their positions and defeat the Federalists.

In 1796, after two terms as president, a weary George Washington decided to retire. In his farewell address, he warned the nation's leaders not to divide the government by forming political parties. They did not listen.

John Adams was elected president in 1796, defeating Jefferson, who became vice president, by a few electoral votes. Adams, a Federalist, joined with Federalists in Congress in backing a law called the Sedition Act. This law established harsh penalties for speaking or writing against the government.

Jefferson saw the law as an attack against freedom of speech, which the First Amendment to the Constitution was meant to protect. He and his close friend James Madison wrote resolutions that were approved by the legislatures of Virginia and Kentucky. The resolutions declared that the national government was the result of a compact, or agreement, among the states. As a result, whenever "the general government assumes undelegated powers," the states have the power to declare the action "void, and of no force."

This marked the introduction of the principles of states' rights, the idea that the power of state governments should be greater than that of the federal government—a basic position of the Democratic Party for decades to come.

Vice President Jefferson began to formally organize his supporters, and by 1800, the Democratic-Republicans had formed. Historians call the existence of the Democratic-Republicans and the Federalists the first American two-party system. Later, the Federalists died out and other parties took their place in opposing the Democrats, as Democratic-Republicans eventually came to call themselves. Today's Democratic Party can trace its roots back to the Democratic-Republicans of Thomas Jefferson.

The 1800 presidential election was a bitter contest between Thomas Jefferson and his Democratic-Republicans and John Adams and the Federalists. Newspapers at the time made no show of impartiality. Editors belonged to one party or another, and what they published clearly reflected the views of their party. In fact, editors did not hesitate to criticize political opponents in the most extreme language. Journalist James Thomson

### NAMING THE PARTY

Thomas Jefferson and his supporters first called themselves Republicans. They took this name, they said, because they opposed government by aristocrats, which is what the Federalists wanted. Federalists then added the tag "Democrats" to Jefferson's group, implying that he and his backers favored mob rule. Eventually the party came to be called the Democratic-Republicans.

Callender wrote in 1801:

> *[John Adams is] that strange compound of ignorance and ferocity, of deceit and weakness ... [who] has neither the force and firmness of a man, nor the gentleness and sensibility of a woman. ... Take your chance between Adams, war, and beggary, and Jefferson, peace, and competency.*

The popular vote showed the relative strength of the two parties in various areas of the country. Jefferson received few votes in New England but many in the South and the Mid-Atlantic states of New York, New Jersey, and Pennsylvania. Most of his votes, though, came from more rural farming areas. Adams, on the other hand, dominated not just New England but also the cities along the coast in the rest of the country. These areas were more business-oriented, reflecting the interests of the Federalists.

John Adams lost the election, but that did not mean that Jefferson was president. At the time, when electors cast their electoral votes, they did not indicate whether they were voting for president or vice president. Just as many Democratic-Republican electors cast their votes for Aaron Burr, the party's candidate for vice president, as they did for Jefferson. As a result, Jefferson and his running mate finished in a tie. That meant the final decision on who should be chosen president was left to the House of Representatives to decide, as required by the U.S. Constitution.

The Federalists in the House had the votes to decide the issue. They looked to Alexander Hamilton, their leader, for guidance. Hamilton disliked Jefferson and disagreed with him strongly, but he despised and feared Aaron Burr. He told his allies to cast their votes for Jefferson, and as a result, Jefferson gained the presidency.

For the next 24 years, a succession of Democratic-Republicans served as president. Thomas Jefferson, James Madison, and James Monroe each served two terms in the White House. During this time, the Democratic-Republicans became the dominant force in American politics.

*James Monroe was the fourth Virginian to serve as president in the nation's first decades. The other three were George Washington, Thomas Jefferson, and James Madison.*

## THE TIE-BREAKER

Soon after the 1800 election, Congress passed the 12th Amendment, which was ratified in 1804. This change to the Constitution prevented the kind of electoral-vote tie between two candidates of the same party that had occurred in 1800 from ever happening again. The amendment stated that electors should each cast one electoral vote for president and one for vice president. The person with the majority in each electoral contest would then be declared the winner for that particular office.

The Federalists, in turn, declined in popularity, in part because they opposed American entry into the War of 1812. Though that war did not produce an American victory—it was more of a draw—it did produce a surge of patriotic feeling among Americans. As a result, the Federalists' opposition to the war helped discredit them. ◣

# The Jacksonian Democratic Party

By the time James Monroe became president in 1817, most politicians were Democratic-Republicans. Historians sometimes call this period the Era of Good Feelings, because political disagreements were at a minimum. Still, there were divisions within the party. Over the next few years, those divisions would overwhelm the good feelings, and out of the resulting turmoil the true Democratic Party would be born.

The first cracks in party unity came in the 1824 election. A group of party legislators picked William Crawford of Georgia, the secretary of the treasury, as the party's candidate. Then various state legislatures weighed in, choosing three other candidates. When the presidential election results were in, Senator Andrew Jackson of Tennessee had the most electoral votes, but he did not have a majority of them. Thus the choice of president was sent to the House of Representatives. One of the four candidates, Henry Clay of Kentucky, told his supporters in the House to vote for the man who had finished second to Jackson, John Quincy Adams of Massachusetts.

*Supporters of Andrew Jackson, who was nicknamed "Old Hickory," proclaimed their candidate a man of the people, although he was actually a wealthy plantation owner.*

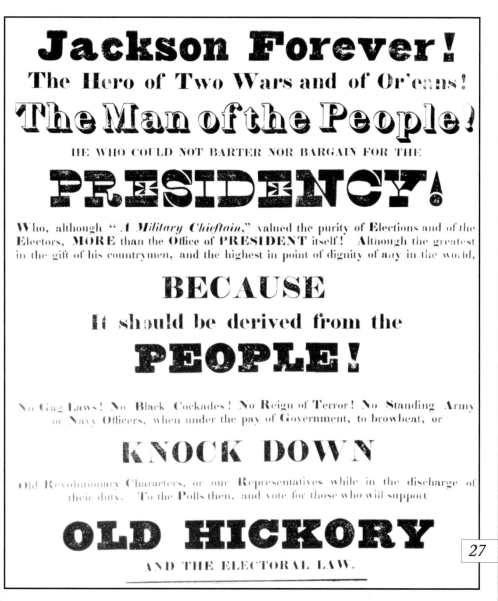

# Jackson Forever!
## The Hero of Two Wars and of Or'eans!
# The Man of the People!
### HE WHO COULD NOT BARTER NOR BARGAIN FOR THE
# PRESIDENCY!

Who, although "*A Military Chieftain*," valued the purity of Elections and of the Electors, **MORE** than the Office of **PRESIDENT** itself! Although the greatest in the gift of his countrymen, and the highest in point of dignity of any in the world,

# BECAUSE
## It should be derived from the
# PEOPLE!

No Gag Laws! No Black Cockades! No Reign of Terror! No Standing Army or Navy Officers, when under the pay of Government, to browbeat, or

# KNOCK DOWN

Old Revolutionary Characters, or our Representatives while in the discharge of their duty. To the Polls then, and vote for those who will support

# OLD HICKORY
### AND THE ELECTORAL LAW.

Adams became president, while Jackson's supporters fumed. Their anger grew stronger when Adams named Clay as his secretary of state. Jackson supporters then claimed that a "corrupt bargain" had given the presidency to Adams. One Jacksonian newspaper published a symbolic death notice for the nation:

> *Expired at Washington on the 9th of February, of poison administered by the assassin hands of John Quincy Adams ... and Henry Clay, the virtue, liberty, and independence of the United States.*

Jackson resigned his Senate seat later in 1825 in order to campaign for the next presidential election.

When the United States was formed, only white men who owned property were allowed to vote. Property owners feared that those who did not own property might demand radical change, threatening the property of those who were better off. Those voting restrictions changed during the 1820s, when many states passed laws extending the right to vote to those who did not own property.

## GAINING THE RIGHT TO VOTE

The reforms of the 1820s did nothing to change the status of women and members of minority groups who were not allowed to vote. African-Americans did not win the right to vote until 1870, after the Civil War. Women did not gain the right to vote until 1920. Not until 1924 did Congress pass a law giving Native Americans the vote. Some Asian-Americans were denied citizenship—and thus the right to vote—until the 1950s. Young people ages 18 to 21 gained the right to vote in 1971.

Jackson benefited from this change. The common men who made up this new group of voters turned out in droves to support him. Three times as many people voted in 1828 as had in 1824, and Jackson won a substantial majority of these votes. He dominated Adams in the electoral college, 178 to 83, to finally become president.

Jackson's presidency helped to shape the Democratic Party. Henry Clay, who had helped Adams win election in 1824, had long backed a program he called the American System. It included the creation of a national bank, passage of high tariffs on imported goods to protect American industries, and the use of government money to build canals and roads to improve transportation.

*Chief Justice John Marshall administered the oath of office to Andrew Jackson on March 4, 1829.*

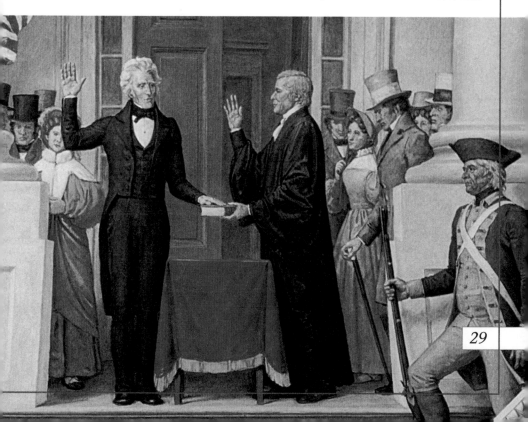

Clay and others who agreed with him began to call themselves National Republicans. This name suggested their preference for a strong national government. Jackson and his supporters still called themselves Democratic-Republicans. Like Jefferson, they favored greater power for the states.

The two groups clashed over the Bank of the United States. Jackson thought it was a tool of businessmen, an enemy of ordinary people, and a violation of the U.S. Constitution. He vowed to destroy it and began pulling the government's deposits out of the bank in order to weaken it.

Clay and his allies hoped to set up Jackson for a loss in the 1832 election by forcing a showdown on the bank issue. Congress passed a bill renewing the bank's charter, which Clay hoped Jackson would veto. He hoped to use that veto to defeat Jackson in the 1832 election.

In vetoing the bill, Jackson claimed to be helping the common man. He said the bank helped only the wealthy and claimed:

> *[It does nothing for] the humble members of society—the farmers, mechanics, and laborers—who have neither the time nor the means of securing like favors to themselves.*

With the bank disagreement as a backdrop, Democratic-Republicans convened in Baltimore, Maryland, in late May 1832. This marked the first national convention of the Democratic Party, a name the group adopted at that time. The convention gladly endorsed Jackson for president and chose New York's Martin Van Buren as his running mate.

*Martin Van Buren was born in Kinderhook, New York. Clubs supporting him during his campaign were called "OK clubs" for the initials of Old Kinderhook. Soon OK came to mean "all right."*

At the convention, the Democrats set two rules that would govern their party meetings well into the 1900s. The first, called the unit rule, established that all of a state's votes were given to the candidate or position that the majority of the delegation supported. For example, if 26 New York delegates out of 50 supported Jackson, then Jackson won all 50 delegates. The second rule established that two-thirds of all the delegates' votes—not a simple majority—were needed in order to nominate a candidate. These rules would later cause problems for the party.

The National Republicans picked Henry Clay as their presidential candidate. Clay's supporters called Jackson "King Andrew the First" and accused him of trampling on the Constitution. But the bank issue worked in Jackson's favor. Tens of thousands of voters agreed with the president that the bank helped only the wealthy. Once again, Jackson won an overwhelming electoral victory— 219 votes to 49.

Two years later, the National Republicans adopted a new name, calling themselves the Whig Party. The contest between the Democrats and Whigs became known as the second American two-party system.

For the next 24 years, Democrats dominated that contest. Jackson's second-term vice president, Martin Van Buren, was elected to the presidency in 1837 and was followed, after four years of Whig

## Naming the Whigs

When the National Republicans changed their name to the Whigs, they were claiming a connection to the patriots who had won American independence. In 1776, Washington, Adams, Jefferson, and others like them called themselves Whigs. They took the name from a British party that opposed excessive royal power, which they believed they were also doing. By taking this name in the 1830s, the Whigs were both linking themselves to the nation's founders and suggesting that their foe, Andrew Jackson, was guilty of claiming too much power.

control, by James K. Polk of North Carolina. After another brief Whig interlude, New Hampshire's Franklin Pierce became president in 1853 and was followed in 1857 by James Buchanan. From 1837 to 1861, the Democrats controlled the White House all but eight years, had a majority in the House of Representatives for all but eight years, and ran the Senate for all but four years. They developed a strong party organization, both in the states and nationally.

By this point, the Democratic Party had come to appeal to voters in all parts of the country. In the North, Democrats won the votes of immigrants and laborers who lived and worked in the cities. West of the Appalachian Mountains, they won the support of farmers. In the South, they were the dominant party in large part because they were committed to protecting slavery, an important issue there. The Democrats' support for slavery would become an increasing burden on the party during the 1840s and 1850s. ◗

# The Fight Over Slavery

**Chapter**

**4**

The South depended on slavery for its economy and built its society around white control of African-Americans. As a result, protecting slavery became a major issue for Southern politicians. In the late 1840s, politicians began to focus on the spread of slavery to territories west of the Mississippi River. Those in the South wanted to see some of these areas become slaveholding states. Politicians in the free states, where slavery did not exist, opposed the expansion of slavery. These two positions ended up destroying the second American two-party system. Southern Whigs moved to the Democratic Party, which supported slavery, and Northern Whigs drifted to other parties.

A bill introduced in Congress in 1854 launched a chain of events that would fracture the Democratic Party as well. The bill became the Kansas-Nebraska Act, and its author was Democratic Senator Stephen Douglas of Illinois.

Douglas wanted to organize the territories of Kansas and Nebraska so the land could be settled, but he faced a dilemma. An 1820 law, the Missouri Compromise, banned slavery in these areas. To win the support of Southerners, Douglas wrote a bill that would repeal the Missouri Compromise. When Congress passed the law, many Northerners howled in protest. Many former Whigs—and the few antislavery Democrats—joined to form a new party, the Republican Party.

*Illinois Senator Stephen Douglas was called the Little Giant because of the combination of his short stature and political power.*

In 1856, the two-year-old Republican Party put forth a candidate for president, John C. Frémont. The Democrats picked James Buchanan of Pennsylvania, an experienced politician. Buchanan won the election, but Frémont won the electoral votes of all but five of the free states, a remarkable showing for an inexperienced candidate leading a new party.

In 1858, antislavery settlers outnumbered pro-slavery ones in Kansas. The pro-slavery forces, however, used deception and trickery to write a state constitution guaranteeing that slavery would be allowed in Kansas even if the majority of residents did not want it. Buchanan urged Congress to admit Kansas as a state based on this constitution. Republicans called this constitution the Great Swindle, and many free-state Democrats agreed. Even Senator Douglas of Illinois, the author of the 1854 Kansas-Nebraska Act, voted against it.

That vote came back to haunt Douglas. In April 1860, the Democrats held their national convention in Charleston, South Carolina.

## THE KNOW-NOTHINGS

Another new party was formed in the 1850s and threatened for a time to be the chief opposition party to the Democrats. It was called the Know-Nothing Party, and its main issue was not slavery but laws against immigrants. The party was formed by nativists who wanted to limit immigration because they feared losing their jobs to these new arrivals. Know-Nothing candidates won several state offices in the free states in the early 1850s and took dozens of seats in the U.S. House as well. By the late 1850s, however, the issue of slavery had come to dominate American politics, and the Know-Nothings moved on to other parties.

*James Buchanan, like several other Democratic presidents in the decades before the Civil War, came from the North but followed policies that supported slavery.*

Remembering Douglas' vote against the pro-slavery Kansas constitution, Southern Democrats refused to nominate him for president. Delegates also clashed over the party's platform. At one point, delegates from free states pushed through a statement on slavery that Southerners did not like. Fifty delegates from the South stormed out of the convention hall. A reporter described the scene:

> *As one followed another in quick succession, one could see the entire crowd quiver as under a heavy blow. Every man seemed to look anxiously at his neighbor as if inquiring what is going to happen next. Down many a manly cheek did I see flow tears of heartfelt sorrow.*

37

*The 1860 Democratic National Convention was marked by anger over the issue of slavery.*

The remaining delegates voted to adjourn for six weeks and try again. The second convention, in Baltimore, Maryland, was worse. This time an even larger number of delegates walked out. Those who remained nominated Stephen Douglas, but he was the candidate of a fractured party. Soon after, Southern Democrats chose their own nominee, Vice President John C. Breckinridge of Kentucky. The Democratic Party had split in two.

Divisions among the Democrats handed the presidency to the Republican candidate, Abraham Lincoln, who easily won an electoral majority. Republicans also won enough seats in the House and Senate to have majorities in both houses of Congress.

The election of Lincoln prompted people in seven Southern states to secede, or withdraw from the Union. These states then formed the Confederate States of America. Soon after, in April 1861, Confederate forces attacked a Union fort, launching the Civil War. Many Northern Democrats immediately rallied to the Union cause. But when Lincoln called for troops to put down the rebellion, four more Southern states left the Union for the Confederacy.

At first, Lincoln's goal was simply to restore the Union. In September 1862, however, he announced a new policy: freeing the slaves in the rebelling states. This new policy turned many Democrats against the war. Horatio Seymour, the Democrat running for governor of New York, declared:

> *If it be true that slavery must be abolished to save this Union, then the people of the South should be allowed to withdraw.*

During the next two years, Democrats became increasingly vocal in criticizing Lincoln's handling of the war. They blasted him for closing newspapers that disagreed with his policies. They complained about the decision to create a draft, in which men were forced to join the Army. They protested when Lincoln announced that he would accept African-American volunteers in the armed forces. Republicans called these Democratic critics Copperheads, after a poisonous rattlesnake.

39

## CLEMENT VALLANDIGHAM

Ohio Democrat Clement Vallandigham (1821–1871) was a leading Copperhead. Born in the South, he bitterly opposed the Civil War and frequently spoke out against Lincoln's policies. Speeches he made in Ohio led a Union general to have him arrested for expressing sympathy for the enemy, and a military court found him guilty. President Lincoln changed his sentence from imprisonment to exile, forcing Vallandigham to flee to the South. Soon after, however, he made his way to Canada, where he continued to speak out against Lincoln's policies. In time, Vallandigham came back to the United States and tried to help the Democrats win the 1864 presidential election. He died on June 17, 1871, by accidentally shooting himself during a demonstration of how a person may have accidentally shot himself.

Some Democrats did continue to support the war effort. One of these so-called War Democrats was picked by Lincoln as his running mate in 1864. He was Andrew Johnson of Tennessee, the only senator from a Confederate state who had not given up his seat in the Senate.

In 1864, Democrats chose George McClellan as their candidate to run against President Lincoln. McClellan had once commanded the main Union Army and had been wildly popular with his troops. With this candidate, the Democrats hoped to win the votes of the Army's soldiers, who they believed were tired of fighting. The party's platform hinted that it would end emancipation and boldly called for an end to the war:

> *After four years of failure to restore the Union by the experiment of war ... justice, humanity, liberty, and the public welfare demand that immediate efforts be made for a cessation of hostilities ... [so that] peace may be restored on the basis of the Federal Union of the States.*

During the summer and fall, however, Union armies won important victories. As a result, Lincoln won re-election, and Republicans gained large majorities in both houses of Congress.

After the Civil War ended in 1865, the Republican Party controlled Reconstruction, the process by which the Southern states were brought back into the Union. It was a difficult time, marked by violence and turmoil in the South. Federal troops were sent there to maintain order.

In the 1876 election, Republican Rutherford B. Hayes of Ohio defeated Democrat Samuel Tilden of New York by one electoral vote. Democrats, however, challenged the electoral votes in three of the Southern states. Congress created a commission to settle the dispute, and the members voted strictly along party lines to rule in favor of Hayes. At the same time, Republican leaders told Southern Democrats that if they accepted Hayes' election, the new president would withdraw the federal troops still stationed in Southern states. The Democrats agreed, and Hayes won the electoral votes. Within two months, the last federal troops had left the South. Reconstruction was over. ◣

# A Push for Reform

The Republican Party was the dominant party in the country from the end of the Civil War until 1933. In those 68 years, Republicans held the presidency for 52 years, led the House for 42 years, and led the Senate for 58 years.

While the Republicans dominated national politics, the Democrats remained strong in some areas. Gradually, white Southerners who had fought for the Confederacy regained control of state governments in the South. The Democratic Southern governments began passing segregation laws that put whites and blacks in separate schools, parks, railroad cars, and other public facilities. Other new laws created barriers that blocked African-Americans from voting, preventing them from pushing the whites out of power.

Democrats also became the chief party in many cities. There they built powerful political organizations known as machines, which were led by people called bosses. The machines thrived by helping immigrants. They helped immigrants get work and provided other services to ensure the immigrants' loyalty. They also registered immigrants to vote—and made sure they voted Democratic.

Many bosses used their positions to become wealthy by taking bribes or kickbacks. The most notorious boss was William Tweed of New York City. "Boss" Tweed and his allies took millions of dollars from the city for themselves. When newspapers published details of the corruption, prosecutors went after Tweed and his followers. They were arrested, tried, convicted, and thrown in prison.

*William "Boss" Tweed controlled New York City's Democratic Party machine and used that power to put friends and associates in many city offices—and to become wealthy.*

43

Tweed was hardly the only corrupt city boss. After he was imprisoned, the Democratic political machine in New York City was simply taken over by someone else. Other bosses ruled other cities, and some were Republicans.

By the 1890s, the working class was facing harsh economic conditions. A new third party arose to try to unite these hard-hit people behind calls for reform. The Populist Party wanted to end the bosses' control of political parties. Populists also wanted the government to regulate the railroads, because the high prices the railroads charged to carry freight hurt farmers. Finally, the Populists wanted the nation to coin more silver money, rather than gold, because silver was more plentiful. This would bring down the value of money and help people like farmers pay off their debt with cheaper dollars.

## THE DEMOCRATIC DONKEY

The donkey—the unofficial symbol of the Democratic Party—became popular in the years after the Civil War. In 1870, political cartoonist Thomas Nast used a drawing of a donkey to criticize some Democratic newspapers. Later he used it to lampoon Democrats in other cartoons. Eventually the donkey became the accepted symbol of the party. Nast also popularized the elephant as the symbol of Republicans. A modern-day Democrat explained the two parties' views of the animals: "The Democrats think of the elephant as bungling, stupid, pompous and conservative—but the Republicans think it is dignified, strong and intelligent. On the other hand, the Republicans regard the donkey as stubborn, silly and ridiculous—but the Democrats claim it is humble, homely, smart, courageous and loveable."

In 1892, the Populist presidential candidate lost to Democrat Grover Cleveland, who, having served as president from 1885 to 1889, now began a second, nonconsecutive term. In 1896, the Populists were prepared to try again, but the Democrats surprised them. William Jennings Bryan of Nebraska, only 36 years old, gave an impassioned speech at the Democratic convention calling for the party to support silver money. It ended with a stirring conclusion:

> *We will answer their [the Republicans'] demand for the gold standard by saying to them: You shall not press down upon the brow of labor this crown of thorns, you shall not crucify mankind upon a cross of gold.*

*In an 1870 political cartoon, Thomas Nast used the donkey to criticize Democrats for their attacks on Edwin Stanton, a Republican leader who had just died.*

The speech thrilled the crowd and won Bryan the presidential nomination. The Populists, hoping to unite their forces with the Democrats, also nominated Bryan. But the two groups were not strong enough to beat the well-run, well-funded campaign of Republican William McKinley.

Prosperity returned under McKinley, and the United States gained colonies with its victory in the 1898 Spanish-American War. These triumphs

*William Jennings Bryan—called the Great Communicator—electrified crowds with his speeches. He was nominated by the Democrats for president three times, but he lost all three elections.*

helped the Republicans defeat Bryan once again in 1900. By this time, silver was a dead issue, and the Populist Party had disappeared. Meanwhile, the new Progressive movement had mounted another push for reform. Progressives picked up several of the government-reform ideas that the Populists had proposed and also wanted to limit the power of large corporations. McKinley's successor as president, Republican Theodore Roosevelt, adopted many of the Progressives' goals. So did Democrat Woodrow Wilson, the governor of New Jersey, who won the presidency in 1912 when the Republican Party split. He was the first Democrat to be elected president in nearly three decades.

During Wilson's presidency, Congress put in place many Progressive ideas. It lowered tariffs to cut the prices on manufactured goods and passed a graduated income tax, meant both to raise revenue and to force the wealthy to shoulder a larger share of the tax burden. Congress also passed the 19th Amendment, which gave women the right to vote. The amendment was ratified in 1920.

Also during Wilson's presidency, World War I broke out in Europe. Wilson tried to keep the United States out of the war, although his policies favored Britain and France over their foes, Germany and Austria. In 1916, Wilson won re-election with the slogan "He kept us out of the war." During his second term, however, Germany resumed submarine attacks on American merchant ships, and an angry public clamored for a declaration of war.

*When Woodrow Wilson took office in 1913, he became the first Democratic president in nearly three decades. He and Grover Cleveland were the only two Democrats to serve as president from 1861 to 1933.*

Though the United States took part in the war for less than two years, fresh American troops played an important role in helping Britain and France win. After the war, Wilson tried to shape the peace. He hoped to create an international body, the League of Nations, that could be used to settle disputes between nations and avoid war. Some people objected to the plan, though, because they felt that joining the league would force the United States to accept the settlement of disputes by other powers. They complained that this meant the country would lose its power to act in its own interests.

As the Senate considered whether to approve the treaty forming the League of Nations, Wilson launched a national campaign to drum up support for his plan. During this time, however, he suffered a stroke and was forced to return to the White House. Eventually the Senate rejected the treaty.

Three Republican presidents followed Wilson into the White House: Warren Harding, Calvin Coolidge, and Herbert Hoover. After the turmoil of Progressive reforms and the excitement of the war, the American people wanted to settle down to a quieter life. Business began to boom, and the 1920s became a time of apparent prosperity and good times. When Hoover took office in 1929, he said that the United States was on the verge of eliminating poverty. He was in for a big surprise.

## THE LONG CONVENTION

The 1924 Democratic convention set all records for length. The meeting opened with a fight over the platform that lasted four days. Then it moved to the task of choosing a candidate. Neither of the two chief contenders—Governor Al Smith of New York or William McAdoo of California—could muster two-thirds of the delegates' votes, as party rules required. Finally, after 103 fruitless votes spread over six days, the Democrats chose John Davis, a lawyer from West Virginia. Soon after, the Democrats abandoned the two-thirds rule.

# The New Deal and the Fair Deal

Chapter

6

Before the end of Herbert Hoover's first year in office, the nation had plunged into its worst economic crisis in history, the Great Depression. Many businesses failed, and others cut back production. Millions of people lost their jobs, and during the worst days of the Depression, a quarter of the work force was unemployed. Banks failed, and people lost their savings. Thousands of families were thrown out of their homes or off their farms because they could not make monthly mortgage payments.

Hoover took some steps to revive the economy, but he did not do much. He did not believe that the government should borrow money in order to create work for the jobless. He also thought the government should not give food to people, even if they were hungry.

*Men who lost their jobs and their homes in the Great Depression stood in line hoping for a place in a shelter.*

Private charities should do this work, he said. As a result, the Depression dragged on throughout Hoover's presidency. As the 1932 election loomed, Democrats saw a great opportunity to win the White House.

For their candidate, the Democrats selected Franklin Delano Roosevelt. A fifth cousin of former President Theodore Roosevelt, he had been the Democratic nominee for vice president in 1920. As governor of New York during the Depression, he had been active in trying to improve the state's economy and help its jobless.

After receiving the party's nomination for president, Roosevelt dramatically broke with tradition by showing up at the convention to speak to the delegates. It was the first time a candidate had ever given a speech accepting the nomination. In it, Roosevelt sounded a theme that would guide his presidency:

*I pledge you, I pledge myself, to a new deal for the American people. Let us all here assembled constitute ourselves prophets of a new order of competence and of courage. This is more than a political campaign; it is a call to arms. Give me your help, not to win votes alone, but to win in this crusade to restore America to its own people.*

The band in the convention hall played a hopeful tune—"Happy Days Are Here Again"—and newspapers quickly gave the name "New Deal" to

*Franklin Roosevelt (waving) established a tradition when he appeared at the 1932 Democratic National Convention to deliver a speech accepting his nomination and launching his campaign.*

Roosevelt's plans and programs. Election Day did bring happy days to the Democrats. Roosevelt won an overwhelming election victory, taking nearly every state in the country.

Roosevelt's election launched a transformation of American politics. He built what is called the New Deal Coalition, which shaped American politics for the next several decades. This alliance included traditional Democratic voters such as farmers, Catholic immigrants, and white Southerners. To these groups, Roosevelt added industrial workers in the cities of the Northeast and Midwest and African-Americans.

*53*

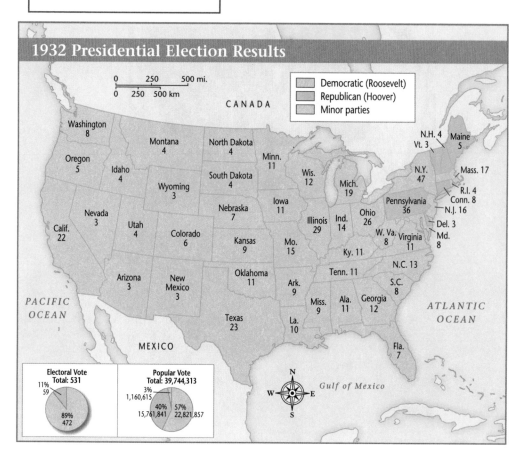

## 1932 Presidential Election Results

0    250    500 mi.
0    250    500 km

CANADA

Democratic (Roosevelt)
Republican (Hoover)
Minor parties

Washington 8
Oregon 5
Idaho 4
Montana 4
North Dakota 4
Minn. 11
South Dakota 4
Wyoming 3
Nebraska 7
Iowa 11
Wis. 12
Mich. 19
N.H. 4
Vt. 3
Maine 5
N.Y. 47
Mass. 17
R.I. 4
Conn. 8
Pennsylvania 36
N.J. 16
Nevada 3
Utah 4
Colorado 6
Kansas 9
Mo. 15
Illinois 29
Ind. 14
Ohio 26
W. Va. 8
Virginia 11
Del. 3
Md. 8
Calif. 22
Ky. 11
N.C. 13
Arizona 3
New Mexico 3
Oklahoma 11
Ark. 9
Tenn. 11
S.C. 8
PACIFIC OCEAN
Texas 23
La. 10
Miss. 9
Ala. 11
Georgia 12
ATLANTIC OCEAN
MEXICO
Fla. 7

**Electoral Vote**
Total: 531
11% 59
89% 472

**Popular Vote**
Total: 39,744,313
3% 1,160,615
40% 15,761,841
57% 22,821,857

N
W E
S
Gulf of Mexico

*Franklin Roosevelt won the presidency by a landslide in the 1932 election.*

On March 4, 1933, Roosevelt took the oath of office in the midst of some of the darkest days of the Depression. Millions of Americans listened to his speech on the radio, hoping that the new Democratic president would offer them help. He began by trying to reassure them:

> *First of all let me assert my firm belief that the only thing we have to fear is fear itself—nameless, unreasoning, unjustified terror which paralyzes needed efforts to convert retreat into advance.*

After the 1933 inauguration, President Roosevelt immediately went to work. In just a few months—a period called the Hundred Days—he got Congress to pass a range of new laws aimed at improving the economy and providing relief for suffering Americans.

Roosevelt's New Deal met a great deal of opposition, though, and not just from Republicans. Many Democrats protested that these radical new programs violated long-standing Democratic values, such as states' rights and limits to federal power. Others worried that increased government spending would hurt, rather than help, the economy. Some critics, however, charged that Roosevelt did not go far enough.

## A DISABLED PRESIDENT

In 1921, at the age of 39, Franklin Roosevelt was stricken by polio. The disease left his legs paralyzed, and he spent the next few years struggling to learn how to manage his disability. For the rest of his life, he had to wear heavy metal leg braces and use crutches or a wheelchair to move. But Roosevelt wanted to project an energetic, confident image as he campaigned for the White House and served as president. As a result, his staff asked reporters not to report his paralysis or take pictures of him in a wheelchair. The press largely complied, and many Americans had no idea that their president could not walk.

Congressional elections in 1934 suggested that Americans liked the New Deal. Typically the president's party loses seats in midterm elections, but that did not happen in 1934. Instead, the Democrats picked up nine seats in both the House and the Senate, giving Roosevelt an even stronger majority. He used that majority to win passage of another flurry of laws, called the Second New Deal.

The New Deal changed the philosophy of the Democratic Party. For the next several decades, the party supported federal government programs that helped ordinary citizens and supported the extra

## MAJOR NEW DEAL PROGRAMS

| Program | Purpose |
| --- | --- |
| Emergency Banking Act | End a banking crisis by providing federal loans to troubled banks |
| Agricultural Adjustment Act (AAA) | Prevent crop surpluses by paying farmers if they agree not to grow crops |
| National Industrial Recovery Act (NIRA) | Revive manufacturing by getting companies and workers to agree on wage, price, and production controls; promote union organizing |
| Federal Relief Act | Provide federal funds to states to help the poor |
| Public Works Administration (PWA), Civil Works Administration (CWA), and Works Progress Administration (WPA) | Provide temporary work to the jobless building roads, schools, and other public facilities |
| Civilian Conservation Corps (CCC) | Provide work to the jobless to improve facilities and national parks and forests |
| Tennessee Valley Authority (TVA) | Build a system of dams and power plants along the Tennessee River to provide power to the region |
| Social Security Act | Provide payments to retired people to encourage older Americans to retire so that younger people will have jobs |

taxes needed to pay for them. From that point on, the term "states' rights," long a core Democratic position, was seldom heard outside the South. There it became a code for racial segregation.

Despite all the programs, Roosevelt could not end the Great Depression. Millions of people did find the relief they needed, and millions went back to work. By the time Roosevelt was elected to a second term in 1936, however, nearly 15 percent of the work force remained unemployed.

In 1940, Roosevelt faced a difficult decision. He had already been president for two terms. Since George Washington had only served two terms, this period was the unofficial limit on one person's being president. But war had already broken out in Europe and Asia, and Roosevelt believed that an experienced leader was needed in the White House. Still, he did not want to openly seek the party's nomination. He wanted the convention to ask him to run. Of course, his campaign managers did everything they could to make sure the convention did just that. The nomination took place as planned, and Roosevelt ran for an unprecedented third term.

Republican presidential candidate Wendell Willkie criticized the president harshly for his decision to run, but most Americans apparently did not mind. Once again, Roosevelt won an easy victory, capturing 38 of 48 states and 449 of 531 electoral votes.

On December 7, 1941, Japan attacked the U.S. naval base at Pearl Harbor, Hawaii, and the United States joined World War II. The war was a difficult two-front battle against Japan in the Pacific and against Germany and Italy in Europe and Africa. Millions of Americans served in the Army and Navy, and industry turned to making guns, planes, tanks, ships, and supplies. The vast output of American factories gave jobs to many people, bringing the Depression to a close.

*The surprise attack at Pearl Harbor on December 7, 1941, caused the United States to declare war on Japan the next day.*

Roosevelt won re-election one more time, in 1944, but by then he was physically worn down. The following spring he died, and the nation mourned the loss of its longtime leader.

Vice President Harry S. Truman then became president. Truman led the nation through the end of World War II and the difficult period of adjustment that followed. To ease that transition, Congress passed a law known as the G.I. Bill of Rights that offered federal aid to help returning veterans pay for a college education and secure low-cost home mortgages. These benefits helped launch a postwar economic boom.

Truman also took steps to end discrimination against African-Americans. In 1948, he issued an executive order banning racial segregation in the armed forces of the United States. These steps further weakened the appeal of the Democratic Party to some white Southerners, who wished to maintain segregation. In 1948, when Truman ran for re-election, several white Southerners bolted from the party and set up their own. They nominated Governor Strom Thurmond of South Carolina for president. Truman dismissed them and focused on his real foe: Republican Thomas Dewey and what he called the "do nothing" Republican Congress. Expected to lose to Dewey, Truman shocked the experts by winning the election.

With his victory, Truman hoped to pass an ambitious program of reforms he called the Fair Deal. However, changing international circumstances forced him to concentrate on foreign policy, as the United States and the Communist Soviet Union began the long struggle for world influence known as the Cold War.

# The 1950s to the 1970s

Chapter

7

During Harry Truman's presidency, a series of unsettling developments occurred in the Cold War. Communist North Korea invaded non-communist South Korea, and American troops were soon fighting to defend the south. China fell to a Communist revolution, and the Soviet Union announced it had developed atomic weapons. Later it became clear that some scientists who had worked on the American atomic-bomb project had given secret information to the Soviets. Some Republicans in Congress charged that Truman's administration was riddled with Communist sympathizers and spies.

Democrats were relieved when Truman announced that he would not run again for the presidency. Still, nominee Adlai Stevenson, the governor of Illinois, had little chance against the Republican candidate, Dwight D. Eisenhower. The popular general had commanded all American, British, and other forces in Europe during World War II. He easily won election as president in 1952 and re-election in 1956.

*A plain-spoken former senator from Missouri, Harry S. Truman was famous for the sign he placed on his White House desk, which read, "The buck stops here."*

*Democratic candidate John F. Kennedy enjoyed a ticker-tape parade in New York City. His glamorous wife, Jacqueline, helped give him a positive image.*

In 1960, Senator John F. Kennedy of Massachusetts, the Democratic candidate, won a close presidential election over Richard Nixon, who had been Eisenhower's vice president. Kennedy was assassinated in November 1963 after serving less than three years. During his time in office, the Cold War claimed most of his energies.

In the 1950s, African-Americans had launched a strong push to gain the civil rights they had long been denied. Kennedy tried to persuade Congress to pass a civil-rights bill to support that effort, but Southern Democrats blocked it. When Kennedy was killed, Vice President Lyndon B. Johnson, a Texan, took office. A skilled politician, he was able to persuade Congress to pass two landmark laws. The Civil Rights Act of 1964 banned discrimination in restaurants, hotels, employment, housing, and other areas of life. The Voting Rights Act of 1965 aimed to block several practices used in the South to deny African-Americans the right to vote.

Johnson's support of civil rights made the Democratic Party an appealing choice for African-American voters but weakened the hold the party had on white voters in the South. Democrats' share of white Southern votes began to shrink in 1964 and continued to grow smaller in later elections.

## THE CATHOLIC PRESIDENT

From the nation's beginning, the majority of people in the United States were Protestants. Many Protestants had deeply negative feelings against Roman Catholics, born of centuries of mistrust. Religious differences spilled into politics as well. Catholics tended to join the Democratic Party, and Republicans were primarily Protestant. For years, experts doubted that a Roman Catholic could ever be elected president. The first to receive a nomination for that office in 1928 was Democrat Al Smith, who lost. The next did not come for 32 years, when Democrats picked John F. Kennedy. During the campaign, Kennedy explained to a meeting of Protestant ministers what he thought of the so-called Catholic issue. He said, "I am not the Catholic candidate for president. I am the Democratic Party's candidate for President who happens also to be a Catholic. I do not speak for my church on public matters, and the church does not speak for me."

*Lyndon Johnson met in his office with four activists from the civil-rights movement. Johnson's political skill led to the passage of landmark civil-rights laws.*

Inspired by the New Deal, Johnson launched an array of programs aimed at ending poverty, improving education, and building what he called the Great Society. In a 1964 speech, he outlined his vision:

> *The Great Society rests on abundance and liberty for all. It demands an end to poverty and racial injustice, to which we are totally committed in our time. But that is just the beginning. The Great Society is a place where every child can find knowledge to enrich his mind and to enlarge his talents. It is a place where leisure is a welcome chance to build and reflect, not a feared cause of boredom and restlessness. It is a place where the city of man serves not only the needs of the body and the demands of commerce, but the desire for beauty and the hunger for community.*

## SOME GREAT SOCIETY PROGRAMS

| Program | Purpose |
| --- | --- |
| Elementary and Secondary Education Act | Provide federal aid to schools in areas with widespread poverty |
| Higher Education Act | Provide federal scholarships to needy students who wish to attend college |
| Medicare, Medicaid | Cover health-care costs for the elderly and the poor |
| Office of Economic Opportunity | End discrimination in employment |
| War on Poverty | Provide welfare benefits to the very poor |
| Job Corps | Give job training to young people who need it |
| Clean Air Act | Reduce air pollution and improve air quality |
| National Endowments of the Arts and Humanities | Fund arts groups and promote culture |

Starting in 1965, Congress passed dozens of new laws that Johnson wanted. Johnson's ambitious programs ran into an obstacle, though. In 1964 and 1965, he dramatically increased American involvement in the Vietnam War, which had begun under Eisenhower and continued under Kennedy. Soon the war consumed much of Johnson's attention, and rising casualty levels dramatically increased opposition to the war at home. Anger over the war led to massive protests involving tens of thousands of people. It led to Johnson's decision not to seek another term and prompted the disastrous 1968 Democratic convention and campaign.

*65*

In the aftermath of the bitter convention of 1968, Democrats set out to reform the party. They enacted a series of measures to wrest control of the party from party bosses and give greater voice to party members. The party also moved to increase the diversity of convention delegates to reflect the racial, ethnic, and gender diversity in the party. As a result, the share of female delegates skyrocketed from 13 percent in 1968 to 40 percent in 1972. The share of African-American delegates tripled.

In 1972, Republican President Richard Nixon was in charge, and the United States was still fighting the Vietnam War. Republicans fully supported Nixon's position on the war—he had brought many troops home, and peace talks were being held. But Democrats were impatient to end the war as soon as possible. They chose Senator George McGovern of South Dakota to run for president. McGovern's platform called unconditionally for peace. He said:

> We believe that war is a waste of human life. We are determined to end forthwith a war which has cost 50,000 American lives, $150 billion of our resources, that has divided us from each other, drained our national will and inflicted incalculable damage to countless people. We will end that war by a simple plan that need not be kept secret: The immediate total withdrawal of all Americans from Southeast Asia.

*Democratic candidate George McGovern was popular in his own party, but he enjoyed little support among the public.*

Richard Nixon, running for re-election, painted McGovern as a wild-eyed liberal who would run away from American responsibilities. Nixon won in a landslide, with McGovern winning the electoral votes of only Massachusetts and the District of Columbia.

Two years later, Nixon was forced to resign because of his role in the Watergate scandal. As facts about the president's involvement in the cover-up became known, Democratic voters began to display a new bumper sticker. It read, "Don't blame me. I voted for McGovern."

Four years later, Democrats could celebrate again. In 1976, Jimmy Carter, a Democrat from Georgia, won the presidential election. Carter symbolized the new kind of Southern Democrat: one comfortable with the civil-rights movement and able to win the support of African-Americans. ◣

*67*

# Democrats in a Republican Age

**Chapter**

**8**

Jimmy Carter had campaigned as an outsider—someone who was not part of the Washington crowd. Once in the capital, though, he was unable to work effectively with members of Congress and other centers of power. Though he enjoyed a Democratic majority in Congress, Carter could not get much of the legislation he wanted passed.

Carter was also plagued by two major problems. First, the Arab oil-producing countries sharply increased oil prices, which badly hurt the American economy. Second, a group of Iranians angry at American support of their former ruler took more than 50 Americans hostage. The hostage crisis dragged on for more than a year. Carter's efforts to use diplomatic and military means to win the release of the hostages failed.

As the 1980 election neared, Americans' approval of Carter's performance was falling steadily. With decreasing popularity, he stood little chance of winning re-election. He faced a stiff challenge from Republican Ronald Reagan. Formerly an actor, Reagan was an effective speaker with an optimistic manner that contrasted with Carter's slow, dull speaking style. Reagan also had a message of hope and was supported by a rising tide of conservatism that was sweeping the country. Reagan won in a landslide.

*Challenger Ronald Reagan (right) surprised President Jimmy Carter by crossing the stage at a televised debate to shake the president's hand.*

Reagan's election signaled the beginning of a new phase of American politics. From 1932 to 1968, Democrats had dominated the presidency, and during that time period, they had controlled Congress most of the time. But Reagan's victory also swept many Republicans into the House and Senate. Though Democrats were still the majority in the House, they lost 33 seats in 1980. The loss of 12 seats in the Senate made them the minority party in that chamber. Over the next quarter century, Republicans came to dominate both the presidency and Congress.

Reagan's election also solidified recent changes in voting patterns. In 1964, Republicans had begun to win the states that had once been seen as the "solid South" of the Democrats. By the time of Reagan's election, these states had become solidly Republican.

## TWO BREAKTHROUGHS

In 1988, the Democratic Party achieved a milestone when it chose a woman, Geraldine Ferraro, for its vice-presidential candidate. During her acceptance speech, Ferraro reminded the convention that slain civil-rights leader Dr. Martin Luther King Jr. had once said, "Occasionally in life there are moments which cannot be completely explained in words. Their meaning can only be articulated by the inaudible language of the heart." Then she added, "Tonight is such a moment for me. My heart is filled with pride." Ferraro, who was Minnesota Senator Walter Mondale's running mate, never got her chance to become the first woman to achieve the office of vice president. Ronald Reagan and George H.W. Bush were re-elected. Twelve years later, Senator Joseph Lieberman won the Democratic Party's nomination for vice president as Senator Al Gore's running mate. Lieberman was the first Jewish person to be nominated for that office.

Another change came in the Northeast and Great Lakes states. These states, home to tens of thousands of immigrants and industrial workers, had been an important part of the New Deal coalition. Many of these voters had flocked to Reagan, however. They, too, became less certain to vote Democratic in future elections.

Reagan had won the election by effectively criticizing Democrats. He claimed that the party was soft on defense, believed in high taxes, and supported a large federal government that took decision-making away from states and local communities. His victory in 1980, and an even larger victory in 1984, convinced many Democrats that they needed to rethink their party's positions.

In 1985, a group of moderate and conservative Democrats formed an organization called the Democratic Leadership Council (DLC). Its goal was to find a new approach to issues that could work in the more conservative atmosphere that prevailed in the country.

DLC members maintained the traditional Democratic goals of equal rights and support for common people. At the same time, they wanted to move the party away from support for big government and business regulation—policies that, they said, hurt ordinary people by slowing economic growth.

In 1992, two members of the DLC—Bill Clinton of Arkansas and Al Gore of Tennessee—won the

Democratic Party nominations for president and vice president. In their campaign, they called for a "third way," rejecting conservative Republican ideas that, they said, ignored government's responsibility to help the people in society who needed help.

They also rejected the traditional Democratic liberalism that viewed government programs as the primary solution to problems. They proposed taking some dramatic steps, such as overhauling the welfare system that had been set up in Johnson's Great Society. They supported free-trade agreements that many labor unions opposed. At the same time, they backed a more traditional Democratic approach to reforming health insurance by involving the government.

*Bill Clinton (right) and Al Gore accepted the acclaim of the delegates at their party's convention.*

Clinton won a narrow victory in 1992, bringing some of the Southern states back into the Democratic fold. Other Democrats were successful as well, and for the first time in 12 years, both the president and the majority of members of Congress belonged to the Democratic Party. Clinton looked forward to what seemed to be an excellent opportunity to tackle the issue of health-insurance reform, but he faced growing opposition to his plan, and it eventually died. His other main issue was the nation's economy, which he tried to improve by working to balance the federal budget. But in 1994, Republicans gained control of the House and Senate. Republican criticism of Clinton's policies convinced the president that he needed to move back to DLC principles. Clinton joined with the Republicans to enact a program to reform the nation's welfare system.

But Clinton also stood up to the Republicans in Congress. They struggled over the federal budget, but Clinton won the fight. Buoyed by this and other successes—as well as a greatly improved economy—Clinton won re-election in 1996. But in the later part of his presidency, he became mired in scandal when he was accused of

## IMPEACHING THE PRESIDENT

Many Republicans in Congress believed that Clinton had lied under oath when testifying about a personal scandal in a court proceeding, and they brought impeachment charges against him. Following the Constitution, the Senate sat in judgment of the president, listening first to the evidence and the arguments. On February 12, 1999, a majority of senators found the president not guilty of perjury, or lying under oath. Though 50 senators found him guilty of obstruction of justice, that was not enough to convict him and remove him from office. Clinton filled out the remainder of his presidency.

trying to hide an inappropriate relationship with a young woman.

In 2000, Vice President Al Gore won the Democratic nomination for president. He was opposed by Republican George W. Bush, the son of George H.W. Bush, who had been president from 1989 to 1993. The election turned out to be one of the closest in American history. Of the more than 105 million votes cast, only about 540,000 votes separated Bush and Gore, a difference of less than one half of 1 percent. The difference was equally close in the electoral college, which Bush won by only one vote.

Bush's victory came in Florida, where questions arose about the accuracy of the vote counts. Gore asked the state to hold a recount, but after it began, Bush sued to stop it, claiming that it was being done in an unfair way.

The case reached the U.S. Supreme Court, which ruled 5 to 4 in favor of Bush. The court's decision stopped the recount and awarded Florida's electoral votes to Republican Bush, making him president. The outcome, which came weeks after Election Day, left a bitter taste in many Democrats' mouths. They pointed out that all five of the justices who voted in favor of Bush had been named to the court by Republican presidents. The ruling, they said, was based on political preferences and not on the law.

Gore decided that he could no longer fight

*Democrats and Republicans argued with each other over the hotly contested election of 2000.*

the election. He made a moving speech accepting the outcome and pledged his support to the incoming president.

Four years later, the Democrats lost a chance to regain the White House. President George W. Bush won re-election against Democratic Senator John Kerry of Massachusetts. The key issue in the election was the war on terrorism that had begun in 2001. Bush convinced voters that he, and not Kerry, would be better able to provide security to Americans. ◣

75

# The Democratic Party Today

The 2004 election divided the country, and the news media's coverage of the contest emphasized that division using color codes made popular in the previous election. States that voted primarily Democratic were identified by the color blue and Republican-voting states by the color red. Today the color blue has joined the donkey as a visual emblem of the Democratic Party.

In 2006, the midterm elections brought more blue to the political map. Voters expressed dissatisfaction with Republican leadership by electing more Democratic candidates to state and federal government offices. Concerns about the budget deficit and the ongoing war in Iraq shifted the balance of power in Washington, giving the Democratic Party control of both the House and the Senate for the first time in 12 years.

*Senator John Kerry of Massachusetts (foreground) and Senator John Edwards of North Carolina could not bring the Democrats back to the White House in 2004.*

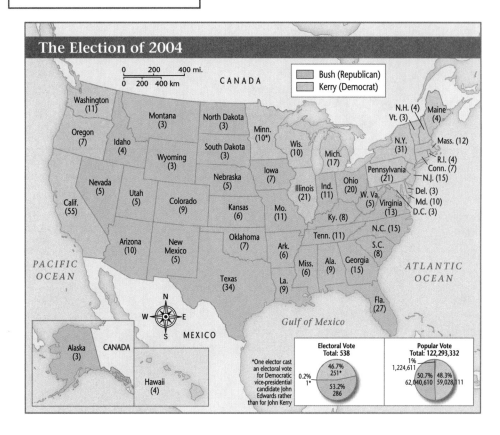

## The Election of 2004

*States in the Northeast and on the West Coast were more likely to vote Democratic in the last presidential election.*

The Democrats gained both legislative chambers in 23 states and improved their position in others. Although most gains came in the Midwest and East, they also gained seats in a few Southern states.

Today's "blue states" are not the same as the Democratic strongholds of the party's early days—the geography of the party has changed greatly over its long history. Democrats no longer count on the South to provide a core of electoral votes. Republicans have been winning in the South for the last several decades and depend on electoral votes from the Great Plains and the West as well. Democrats consistently win in the

Northeast and on the West Coast, but these areas provide fewer electoral votes.

More voters identify themselves as Democrats than Republicans—about 33 percent, compared with about 28 percent. But the difference between the two parties is much smaller than it was in the past. In 1952, nearly 50 percent of Americans said they were Democrats. In the past 50 years, the number of people who identify themselves as members of the party has shrunk by about a third. The largest group of people—nearly 40 percent—call themselves Independents.

Who are the members of the Democratic Party? In the past, most Roman Catholics were Democrats, but that is no longer the case. Today Catholics are evenly split among Democrats, Republicans, and Independents. Jews form the one religious group that identifies mainly with the party—nearly 60 percent are Democrats.

A slightly higher percentage of men are Republicans rather than Democrats, but women Democrats outnumber women Republicans by 37 percent to 28 percent. Among ethnic groups, 61 percent of African-Americans are Democrats, but only 3 percent are Republicans. Thirty-seven percent of Hispanics are Democrats, while only 14 percent are Republicans. Americans with yearly incomes less than $30,000 are twice as likely to be Democrats as Republicans; those who earn more than $90,000 a year are more likely to be Republicans.

About 40 percent of Democrats say they are liberal, and another 50 percent say they are moderate. Only about 10 percent say they are conservative. The opposite is true of the Republican Party. Two-thirds say they are conservative, 30 percent say they are moderate, and only a handful claim to be liberal. Democrats' positions on the issues reveal their more liberal stance, which dates back to the New Deal.

What do these modern-day Democrats believe in? The chart compares Democratic and Republican positions based on statements made in the 2004 party platforms.

| REPUBLICAN AND DEMOCRATIC POSITIONS | | |
|---|---|---|
| Issue | Republican Position | Democratic Position |
| War on terrorism | Fully endorses all actions taken by President Bush, including invasions of Afghanistan and Iraq | Criticizes Bush for invasion of Iraq, which distracted troops from needs in Afghanistan and for alienating possible allies |
| Patriot Act (law that gives law-enforcement officials new tools to investigate possible terrorists) | Act should be extended as originally written, with full powers to law enforcement | Act should be extended with changes to prevent actions that could endanger the civil rights of Americans |
| Federal deficit (need to borrow money because the government spends more than it takes in) | Bush economic policies will help the economy grow, thereby cutting the deficit | Bush policies are responsible for the deficit; taxes on wealthiest people and cuts in spending are needed |
| Taxes | Tax cuts made in first Bush term should be continued to promote economic growth | Tax cuts for the poor and middle class should be continued but not for the wealthiest people |
| Illegal immigrants | Employers who hire illegal immigrants should be punished; illegal immigrants should not be allowed to stay in country | Illegal immigrants with no criminal records who have jobs should be allowed to stay and eventually become citizens |

| Issue | Republican Position | Democratic Position |
|---|---|---|
| Gun control | Second Amendment ensures the right to own guns; best way to control guns is to give harsh penalties to those using guns to commit crimes | Second Amendment ensures the right to own guns, but assault weapons should be banned |
| Social Security | System should allow individuals to control the investment of part of their own contribution | System should not include personal investment |
| Same-sex marriage | A constitutional amendment should define marriage as only involving one man and one woman | This question should be left to individual states |
| Racial discrimination | Discrimination on the basis of race, gender, or any other factor is wrong; any system that sets aside certain numbers of jobs or places in college for members of certain groups is also wrong | Discrimination on the basis of race, gender, or any other factor is wrong; systems that give advantages to racial or gender groups to redress past discrimination are fair |
| Abortion rights | Unborn children are protected by the 14th Amendment; opposes abortion and use of public funds to pay for abortions for poor women | Women's rights to abortion should be protected; public funds should be used to help poor women have the same rights as those with money |
| Health insurance | People should be insured through their employers or by buying their own insurance; cutting costs will make insurance more affordable | People should be insured through their employers or by buying their own insurance; the government should cover the health costs of the poor and provide insurance to children without it |
| Pollution controls | Allowing companies to buy and sell pollution credits is best way to control pollution | Strict pollution controls are needed; any company that causes pollution should pay for cleanup |
| Energy policy | A combination of increased domestic production, investment in alternative sources of energy, and conservation is needed | The Republican policy is based on oil; there needs to be an emphasis on renewable sources of energy and conservation |

81

Today's Democrats are much more likely to favor the government's taking a major role in helping Americans. More than half of Democrats think the government should provide health insurance for all Americans, a position fewer than a quarter of Republicans agree with. More than half of Democrats say they want the government to spend more to provide increased services in health care and education; only a fifth of Republicans agree.

*A group of delegates at the 2004 Democratic National Convention suggests the diversity of the party.*

Democrats are also more liberal than Republicans on social issues. Fewer than half of Democrats are against using government funds to allow poor women who could not otherwise afford it to obtain an abortion. Three-quarters of Republicans oppose that use of federal money. Forty percent of Democrats agree with the idea that homosexuals should be allowed to marry, while only 14 percent of Republicans agree.

In 1972, the Democratic Party platform came out squarely for an end to the Vietnam War and reduced military spending. Since then, Republicans have claimed that Democrats do not support a strong defense. The responses that members of both parties give to public-opinion polls suggest that there are indeed differences between them on national security and defense issues. In a 2004 poll, only 34 percent of Democrats said that military spending should be increased, while 76 percent of Republicans thought so. Democrats are also much less willing than Republicans to go to war. Only 23 percent agreed with the statement that the country "must be ready to use force versus diplomacy to solve international problems." In contrast, 60 percent of Republicans agreed with the statement.

The Democratic Party has changed in some respects since its origin. From its beginning under Thomas Jefferson, the party supported the power of state governments over the federal government. Since the New Deal, however, Democrats have

*83*

tended to rely on the power of the federal government to accomplish their goals. They favor using government spending to stimulate the economy when necessary. They believe the government should implement and manage programs to help the poor and disadvantaged. And they think the federal government, rather than the states, is in the best position to ensure equal treatment of Americans of every race, ethnic group, gender, and religion.

Today's Democrats believe in American diversity. From its early years, the party embraced immigrants and encouraged them to enter the United States and join in American life. For many decades, though, the party was opposed to ending slavery and later, when it was abolished, to granting equal rights to African-Americans. Not until the New Deal of the 1930s did many in the party begin to work for civil rights. Even then, white Southern Democrats tended to oppose those efforts. Today, however, most African-Americans see the Democratic Party as the party that cares most about their concerns. The party once dominated by white slaveholders has evolved into the party of civil rights for minorities, women's rights, and cultural diversity.

One Democratic position, however, shows great continuity with the past. Jefferson wanted his party to help ordinary farmers, which most people were at the time. Later, Andrew Jackson believed that his policies would assist the common man. Today, too, Democrats argue that their policies are best for ordinary working Americans. Presidential candidate Al Gore expressed this idea in 2000:

*My focus is on working families—people trying to make house payments and car payments, working overtime to save for college and do right by their kids ... whether you're in a suburb, or an inner-city ... whether you raise crops or drive hogs and cattle on a farm, drive a big rig on the Interstate, or drive e-commerce on the Internet. ... How and what we do for all of you—the people who pay the taxes, bear the burdens, and live the American dream—that is the standard by which we should be judged.*

Jefferson and Jackson would be surprised by the diversity of the Democratic Party today. But they would not be surprised by Democrats' dedication to making the country better for ordinary people.

# Timeline

**1792**

Thomas Jefferson organizes members of Congress who oppose policies of Alexander Hamilton.

**1798–1800**

Jefferson and his supporters form the Democratic–Republican Party.

**1801–1809**

Jefferson serves as the third president.

**1817–1825**

James Monroe serves as the fifth president; the Era of Good Feelings, in which Democratic–Republicans face little opposition, begins.

**1829–1837**

Andrew Jackson serves as the seventh president.

**May 21, 1832**

The Democratic Party holds its first national convention and adopts the name "Democratic Party."

**1837–1841**

Martin Van Buren serves as the eighth president.

**1845–1849**

James K. Polk serves as the 11th president.

**1853–1857**

Franklin Pierce serves as the 14th president.

**1854**

Congress passes the Kansas–Nebraska Act; the Republican Party forms in the free states.

**1857–1861**

James Buchanan serves as the 15th president.

**April 23–May 3, 1860**

Democrats hold their national convention in Charleston, South Carolina, but fail to agree on a nominee for president.

**June 18–23, 1860**

Democrats hold their second convention and nominate Stephen Douglas for president; Southern Democrats walk out.

**1865–1869**

Andrew Johnson, a Democrat elected as Republican Abraham Lincoln's vice president, serves as the 17th president.

**1870**

Political cartoonist Thomas Nast first uses a donkey to stand for the Democratic Party.

**1885–1889**

Grover Cleveland serves as the 22nd president.

**1893–1897**

Cleveland serves as the 24th president.

**July 7, 1896**

William Jennings Bryan gives his "Cross of Gold" speech and gains the Democratic nomination for president; Bryan loses election to William McKinley.

**1913–1921**

Woodrow Wilson serves as the 28th president.

**July 1, 1932**

On the fourth ballot, the Democratic National Convention nominates Franklin Delano Roosevelt for president; the next day, Roosevelt breaks with tradition by delivering an acceptance speech in person.

**1933–1945**

Roosevelt serves as the 32nd president and launches the New Deal to try to end the Great Depression.

**1945–1953**

After Roosevelt dies in office, Harry S. Truman becomes the 33rd president.

**1961–1963**

John F. Kennedy serves as the 35th president.

**1963–1969**

After Kennedy is assassinated, Lyndon Johnson becomes the 36th president.

**July 2, 1964**

Johnson signs the Civil Rights Act of 1964 into law.

**March 31, 1968**

Johnson announces he will not seek the Democratic nomination for president.

**June 6, 1968**

Robert Kennedy dies from an assassin's bullet two days after winning the California primary.

**August 26–29, 1968**

The Democratic National Convention in Chicago is troubled by turmoil, violence, and conflict within the party.

**November 5, 1968**

Vice President Hubert Humphrey is defeated in the presidential election.

# Timeline

### 1977–1981

Jimmy Carter serves as the 39th president.

### November 4, 1979

Iranian students seize the U.S. Embassy in Iran, taking more than 50 hostages.

### January 20, 1981

As Republican Ronald Reagan is sworn in as president, the hostages in Iran are released.

### July 19, 1984

Democrats nominate Geraldine Ferraro for vice president; Ferraro is the first woman to receive a major-party nomination for president or vice president.

### 1985

Moderate and conservative Democrats found the Democratic Leadership Council.

### 1993–2001

Bill Clinton serves as the 42nd president.

### December 19, 1998

The House of Representatives impeaches Bill Clinton, which would result in his removal from office if he were convicted by the Senate.

### February 12, 1999

Senate votes not to convict Clinton of impeachable offenses.

### December 12, 2000

In *Bush v. Gore*, the U.S. Supreme Court orders the recount of Florida votes stopped, giving the disputed election of 2000 to George W. Bush.

### November 7, 2006

Midterm elections give control of both houses of Congress to the Democrats.

## On the Web

For more information on this topic, use FactHound.

**1** Go to *www.facthound.com*

**2** Type in this book ID: 0756524504

**3** Click on the *Fetch It* button. FactHound will find the best Web sites for you.

## Historic Sites

Franklin Delano Roosevelt Memorial
900 Ohio Drive SW
Washington, D.C. 20024
202/426-6841

This memorial in Washington, D.C., features exhibits about the life of the man who shaped the modern Democratic Party.

The Hermitage
4580 Rachel's Lane
Nashville, TN 37076
615/889-2941

The home of Andrew Jackson features information about his life and ideas.

## Look for more books in this series

**Brown v. Board of Education:**
*The Case for Integration*

**The Chinese Revolution:**
*The Triumph of Communism*

**The Japanese American Internment:**
*Civil Liberties Denied*

**The Indian Removal Act:**
*Forced Relocation*

**The Progressive Party:**
*The Success of a Failed Party*

**The Republican Party:**
*The Story of the Grand Old Party*

**The Scopes Trial:**
*The Battle Over Teaching Evolution*

89

A complete list of **Snapshots in History** titles is available on our Web site: *www.compasspointbooks.com*

# Glossary

**amendment**
formal change to the U.S. Constitution

**bill**
proposed law introduced in Congress that must be passed by both the Senate and the House of Representatives and signed by the president or passed again by both houses of Congress to become law

**boss**
political leader who holds great power by controlling his party's political organization in a city or state

**charter**
document that lays out the legal powers of a particular institution

**coalition**
alliance of people or groups working toward a common goal

**conservative**
opposed to change, preferring to keep things as they are

**executive order**
proclamation by a president that has the force of law

**impeachment**
process for charging a government official with misconduct while in office

**liberal**
favoring progress, reform, and the protection of civil liberties

**midterm**
congressional election that takes place two years after a presidential election

**nativists**
people who want laws giving preferences to native-born Americans and restricting immigration

**nomination**
choosing someone as a candidate for political office

**partisan**
firm adherence to a party, faction, cause, or person

**platform**
statement of political goals made by members of a political party

**primary**
election in which candidates of the same party try to win that party's nomination as candidate for a particular office

**resolutions**
formal expressions of opinion, will, or intent voted on by an official body or assembled group

## SOURCE NOTES

### Chapter 1

Page 10, line 15: Theodore H. White. *The Making of the President 1968*. New York: Atheneum, 1969, p. 90.

Page 10, line 25: Ibid., p. 124.

Page 14, line 9: Ibid., p. 303.

Page 15, sidebar: David M. Kennedy. *Freedom From Fear: The American People in Depression and War, 1929–1945*. New York: Oxford University Press, 1999, p. 31.

### Chapter 2

Page 21, lines 28 and 30: "Kentucky's Resolutions." *The Founders' Constitution, Volume 5, Amendment I (Speech and Press), Document 18, Nov. 14, 1799*. 6 Oct. 2006. http://press-pubs.uchicago.edu/founders/documents/amendl_speechs18.html

Page 23, line 2: Fawn Brodie. *Thomas Jefferson: An Intimate Portrait*. New York: Norton, 1974, p. 321.

### Chapter 3

Page 28, line 4: James A. Henretta, David Brody, and Lynn Dumenil. *America: A Concise History*. Boston: Bedford/St. Martin's, 1999, p. 287.

Page 28, line 8: Paul Boller Jr. *Presidential Campaigns*. New York: Oxford University Press, 1996, p. 37.

Page 30, line 22: Ibid., p. 54.

### Chapter 4

Page 37, line 9: Bruce Catton. *The Coming Fury*. New York: Pocket Books, 1967, p. 34.

Page 39, line 18: James M. McPherson. *The Battle Cry of Freedom*. New York: Ballantine Books, 1989, p. 560.

Page 41, line 1: "Democratic Platform of 1864." *The American Presidency Project*. 6 Oct. 2006. www.presidency.ucsb.edu/showplatforms.php?platindex=D1864

## Source Notes

### Chapter 5

Page 44, sidebar: "History of the Democratic Donkey." The Democratic National Committee. 6 Oct. 2006. www.democrats.org/a/2005/06/history_of_the.php

Page 45, line 9: Peter Levy, ed. *100 Key Documents in American Democracy*. Westport, Conn.: Greenwood Press, 1994, p. 212.

### Chapter 6

Page 52, line 20: *Presidential Campaigns*, p. 233.

Page 54, line 7: *100 Key Documents in American Democracy*, p. 332.

### Chapter 7

Page 63, sidebar: Theodore H. White. *The Making of the President 1960*. New York: New American Library, 1967, p. 439.

Page 64, line 6: *100 Key Documents in American Democracy*, p. 423.

Page 66, line 22: "Democratic Party Platform of 1972." *The American Presidency Project*. 6 Oct. 2006. www.presidency.ucsb.edu/showplatforms.php?platindex=D1972

### Chapter 8

Page 70, sidebar: Colleen McGuiness, ed. *National Party Conventions, 1831–1988*. Washington, D.C.: Congressional Quarterly, 1991, p. 148.

### Chapter 9

Page 83, line 14: Christine Barbour and Gerald C. Wright. *Keeping the Republic: Power and Citizenship in American Politics*. Washington, D.C.: CQ Press, 2006, p. 506.

Page 85, line 7: Al Gore Jr. "Speech Transcript: Acceptance Speech at the 2000 Democratic National Convention." *AlGore.org*. 17 Aug. 2000. 16 Nov. 2006. www.algore.org/index.php?option=com_content&task=view&id=84&Itemid=84

## Select Bibliography

Barbour, Christine, and Gerald C. Wright. *Keeping the Republic: Power and Citizenship in American Politics.* 3rd ed. Washington, D.C.: CQ Press, 2006.

Boller, Paul F., Jr. *Presidential Campaigns.* New York: Oxford University Press, 1996.

Bonadio, Felice A., ed. *Political Parties in American History, Vol. 2: 1828–1890.* New York: Putnam's, 1974.

Henretta, James A., David Brody, and Lynn Dumenil. *America: A Concise History.* Boston: Bedford/St. Martin's, 1999.

McGuiness, Colleen, ed. *National Party Conventions, 1831–1988.* Washington, D.C.: Congressional Quarterly, 1991.

Murphy, Paul L., ed. *Political Parties in American History, Vol. 3: 1890–Present.* New York: Putnam's, 1974.

Reichley, A. James. *The Life of the Parties: A History of American Political Parties.* New York: The Free Press, 1992.

Troy, Gil. *See How They Ran: The Changing Role of the Presidential Candidate.* New York: The Free Press, 1991.

White, Theodore H. *The Making of the President 1968.* New York: Atheneum, 1969.

## Further Reading

Colbert, Nancy A. *Great Society: The Story of Lyndon Baines Johnson.* Greensboro, N.C.: Morgan Reynolds Publishing, 2002.

Collier, Christopher, and James Lincoln Collier. *Andrew Jackson's America: 1824–1850.* New York: Benchmark Books, 1998.

Landau, Elaine. *Friendly Foes: A Look at Political Parties.* Minneapolis: Lerner Publications, 2004.

Ruth, Amy. *Growing Up in the Great Depression, 1929 to 1941.* Minneapolis: Lerner Publications, 2002.

# Index

## ABOUT THE AUTHOR

Dale Anderson studied history and literature at Harvard College. He has worked in publishing ever since. He lives with his wife and two sons in Newtown, Pennsylvania, where he writes and edits textbooks and library books. He has written several books for young adults, including books on the Tet Offensive, the Watergate scandal, and the Republican Party in the Snapshots series.

## IMAGE CREDITS